Counting Feathers

This book is dedicated to:
Karl, Willy, and Bradley – Al
Ira – Brian

Published by
LONGSTREET PRESS, INC.
A subsidiary of Cox Newspapers,
A subsidiary of Cox Enterprises, Inc.
2140 Newmarket Parkway
Suite 122
Marietta, Georgia 30067

Text copyright © 1997 by Al Simmons
Based on the songs "Counting Feathers" and "I Collect Rocks" lyrics by Al Simmons and
music by Ken Whiteley © Branch Group Music Publishing
Illustrations copyright © 1997 by Brian Floca

Produced by Vickey Bolling
Printed by Paramount Printing Company Limited, Hong Kong
The text of this book is set in 20 point Lemonade ICG. The illustrations are
in ink and watercolor on Winsor Newton 140lb CP watercolor paper.

1st Printing, 1997
Library of Congress Card Catalog Number 97-71934
ISBN: 1-56352-440-6

Special thanks to Gilles Paquin and the Oak Street Music label. For more information, contact Oak Street at Paquin@magic.mb.ca

Counting Feathers

Stephens Elementary

Written by Al Simmons
Illustrations by Brian Floca

i think I'll fetch my feather collection
For an annual inspection.

Line them up and organize,
Sort them out by shape and size.
I'm building up an inventory;
Every feather tells a story.

I'm counting feathers one by one,
Counting feathers – I've begun
To pile them up in stacks of ten,
This one, a goose; that one, a hen.

Here's the first feather I found
Just lying there upon the ground.
It's gray and brown and short and narrow;
I think that it came from a sparrow.

A jay dropped this one from a tree
As if it were a gift for me.

I'm counting feathers two by two;
I've got so many more to do.
I bet you I could fill a truck!
Hey, look at this one — thank you, Duck!

I found this on my window sill,
I think it's from a whippoorwill.
This one's from a grouse in flight,
That one's from a pillow fight!

I overheard a seagull screech
And found this lying on the beach.

The black one blew off a crow in a storm,
I hope it can manage to keep itself warm.
The white one's from the caboose of a goose.
It was scratching itself – that's how it came loose.

I'm counting feathers three by three:
Owl, eagle, and chickadee;
Swallow, grosbeak, raven, wren,
Bluebird, blackbird, ptarmigan.
While I was reading the newspaper page,
I found this one inside the parakeet cage.

I'm counting feathers four by four,
I've **never** plucked one, that's for sure.
They fell when the birds were moulting,
Or chased by cats – oh, how revolting!

Quick, close the door! A sudden breeze
Will blow them – **Ooooohhhhhhhhh**...
Here comes a *SNEEZE*...

I guess I'll count them once again,
Pile them up in stacks of ten.
The ostrich plume and blue peacock's –

Hey, I should be collecting **rocks!**

Now I'm collecting stones and rocks;
Loading them into bag and box.

Filling pockets, filling socks, I gain weight,
I'm gaining weight when I take walks!

Volcanic or sedimentary —
How many more rocks can I carry?
I pick up every rock I find.
A gravel road is my gold mine.

From a pebble to a boulder,
I can't wait until I'm older,
So when I go for walks
I can carry lots more rocks!